PARES SCALES

For Individual Study
and Like-Instrument Class Instruction

by GABRIEL PARÈS

Revised and Edited by Harvey S. Whistler

Published for:

Flute or Piccolo . . . . Parès-Whistler

Clarinet . . . . Parès-Whistler

Oboe . . . . Parès-Whistler

Bassoon . . . . Parès-Whistler

Saxophone . . . . Parès-Whistler

Cornet, Trumpet or Baritone 𝄞 . . . . Parès-Whistler

French Horn, E♭ Alto or Mellophone . . . . Parès-Whistler

Trombone or Baritone 𝄢 . . . . Parès-Whistler

● E♭ Bass (Tuba - Sousaphone) . . . . Parès-Whistler

BB♭ Bass (Tuba - Sousaphone) . . . . Parès-Whistler

Marimba, Xylophone or Vibes . . . . Parès-Whistler-Jolliff

For Individual Study and Like-Instrument Class Instruction
(Not Playable by Bands or by Mixed-Instruments)

RUBANK®

HAL•LEONARD®
CORPORATION

7777 W. BLUEMOUND RD P O BOX 13819 MILWAUKEE, WI 53213

Key of C Major

Long Tones to Strengthen Lips

Scale of C

Also practice holding each tone for EIGHT counts.
When playing long tones, practice (1) ⟨ and (2) ⟨⟩ .

993-47

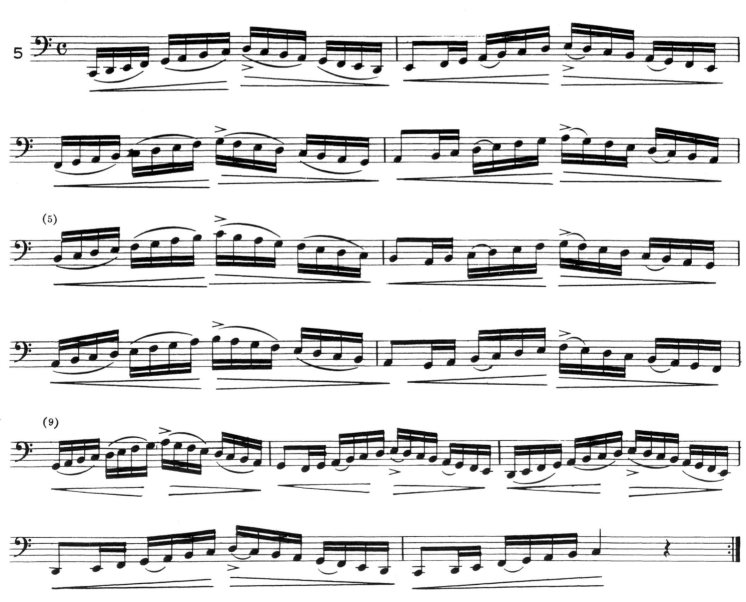

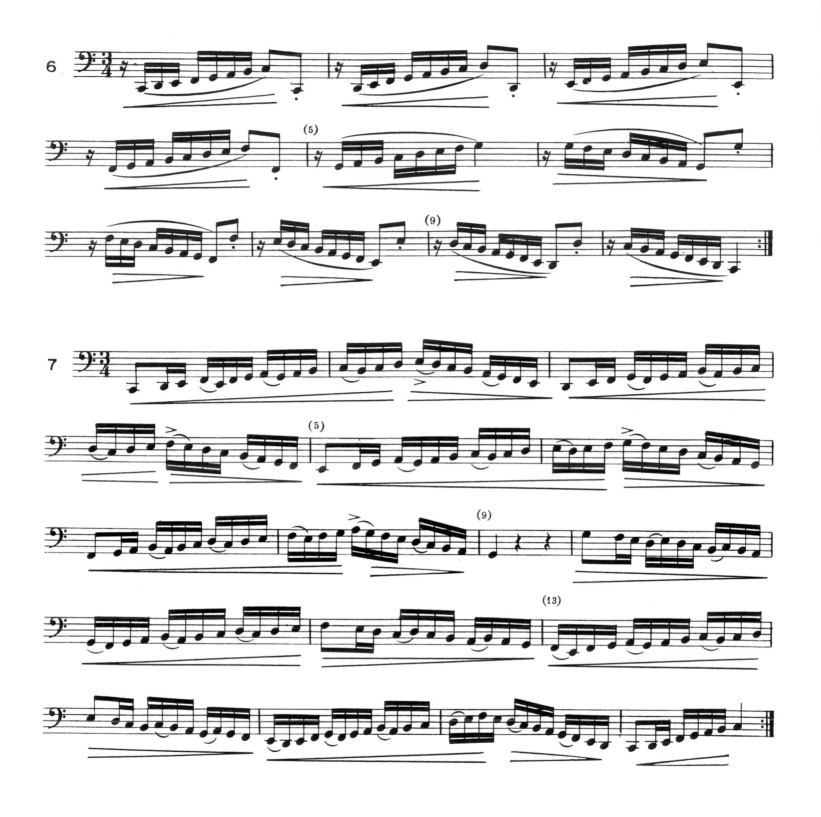

Embouchure Studies

Slur as many tones as possible. Also practice tonguing each tone.

Slur as many tones as possible. Also practice tonguing each tone.

Key of F Major

Long Tones to Strengthen Lips

Scale of F

10

Also practice holding each tone for EIGHT counts.
When playing long tones, practice (1) ⏜ and (2) ⏝.

11

12

13

Embouchure Studies

Slur as many tones as possible. Also practice tonguing each tone.

Slur as many tones as possible. Also practice tonguing each tone.

Key of G Major

Long Tones to Strengthen Lips

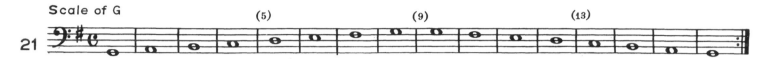

21

Also practice holding each tone for EIGHT counts.
When playing long tones, practice (1) ⟨ and (2) ⟨ ⟩ .

22

23

24

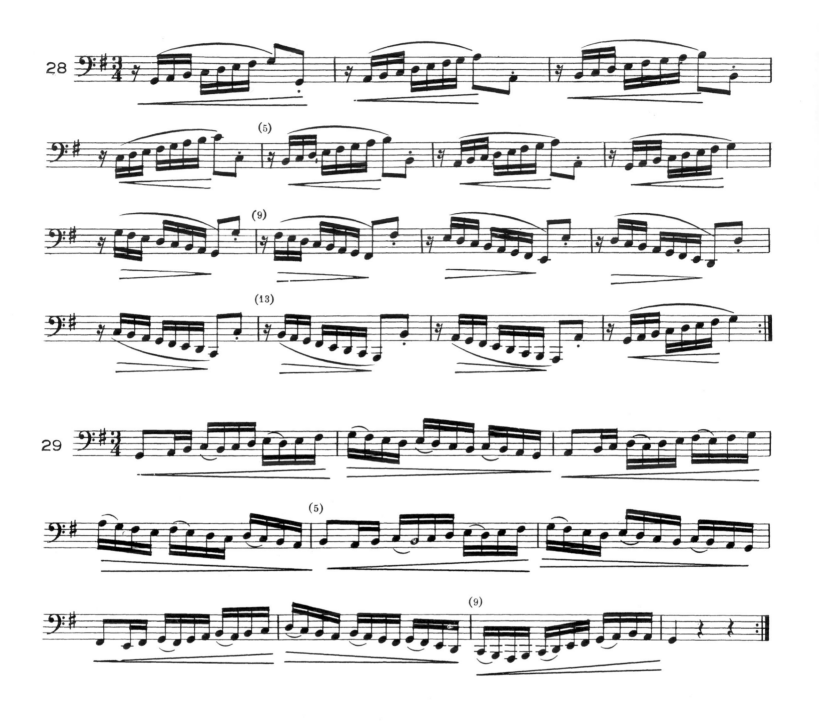

Embouchure Studies

Slur as many tones as possible. Also practice tonguing each tone.

Slur as many tones as possible. Also practice tonguing each tone.

Key of Bb Major

Long Tones to Strengthen Lips

Also practice holding each tone for EIGHT counts.
When playing long tones, practice (1) ⦦ and (2) ⦦⦧ .

36

37

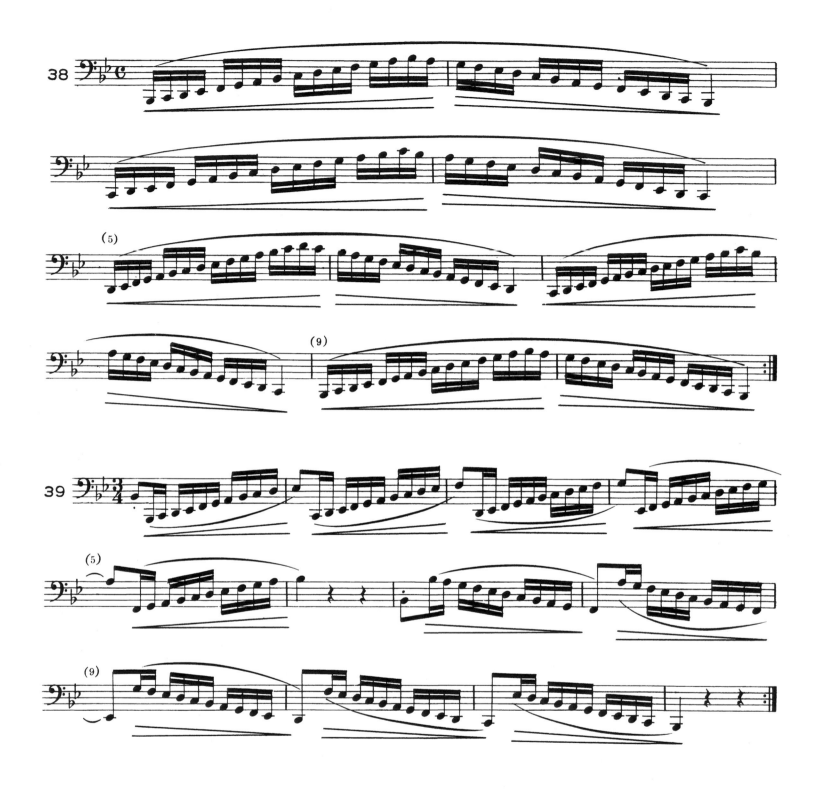

Embouchure Studies

Slur as many tones as possible. Also practice tonguing each tone.

Slur as many tones as possible. Also practice tonguing each tone.

Key of D Major

Long Tones to Strengthen Lips

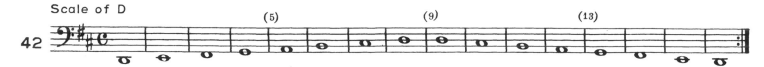

Also practice holding each tone for EIGHT counts.
When playing long tones, practice (1) ⪦ and (2) ⪦⪧ .

993-47

Embouchure Studies

Slur as many tones as possible. Also practice tonguing each tone.

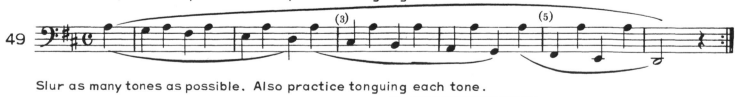

Slur as many tones as possible. Also practice tonguing each tone.

Key of E♭ Major

Long Tones to Strengthen Lips

Also practice holding **each tone** for EIGHT counts.
When playing long tones, practice (1)  and (2) .

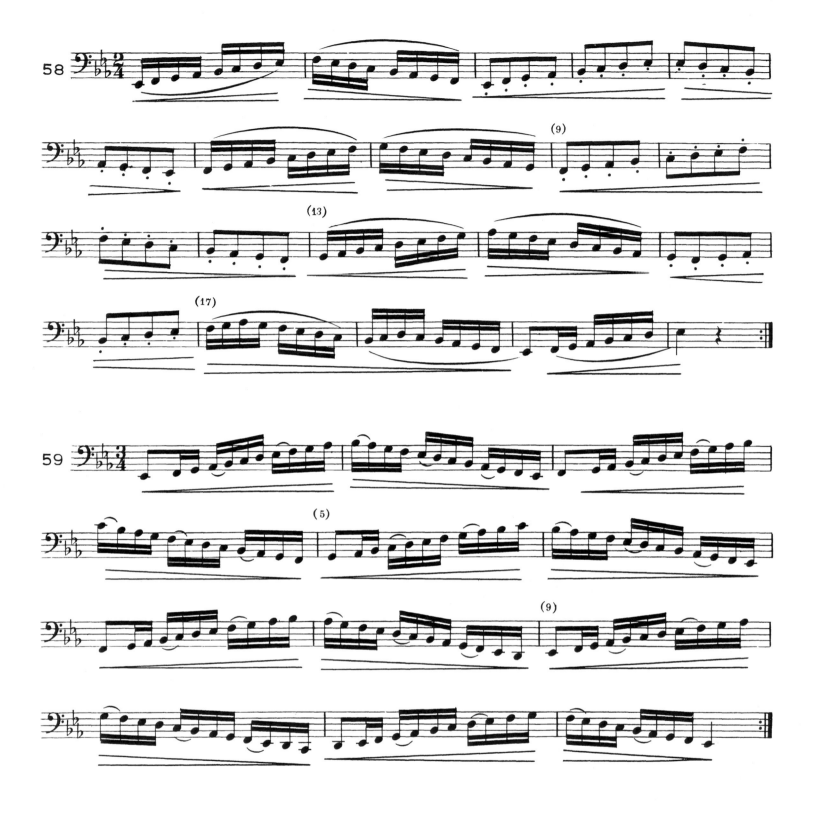

Embouchure Studies

Slur as many tones as possible. Also practice tonguing each tone.

Slur as many tones as possible. Also practice tonguing each tone.

Key of A Major

Long Tones to Strengthen Lips

Also practice holding each tone for EIGHT counts.
When playing long tones, practice (1) ⟨ and (2) ⟨ ⟩ .

Embouchure Studies

Slur as many tonés as possible. Also practice tonguing each tone.

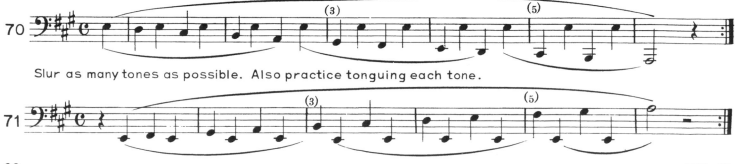

Slur as many tones as possible. Also practice tonguing each tone.

993-47

Key of A♭ Major

Long Tones to Strengthen Lips

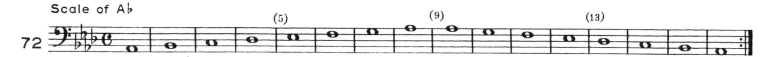

72   Scale of A♭

Also practice holding each tone for EIGHT counts.
When playing long tones, practice (1) ⎯⎯ and (2) ⎯⎯ ⎯⎯ .

73

74

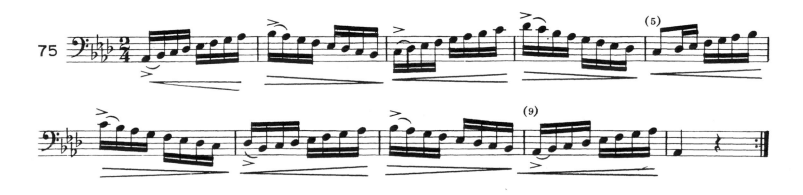

75

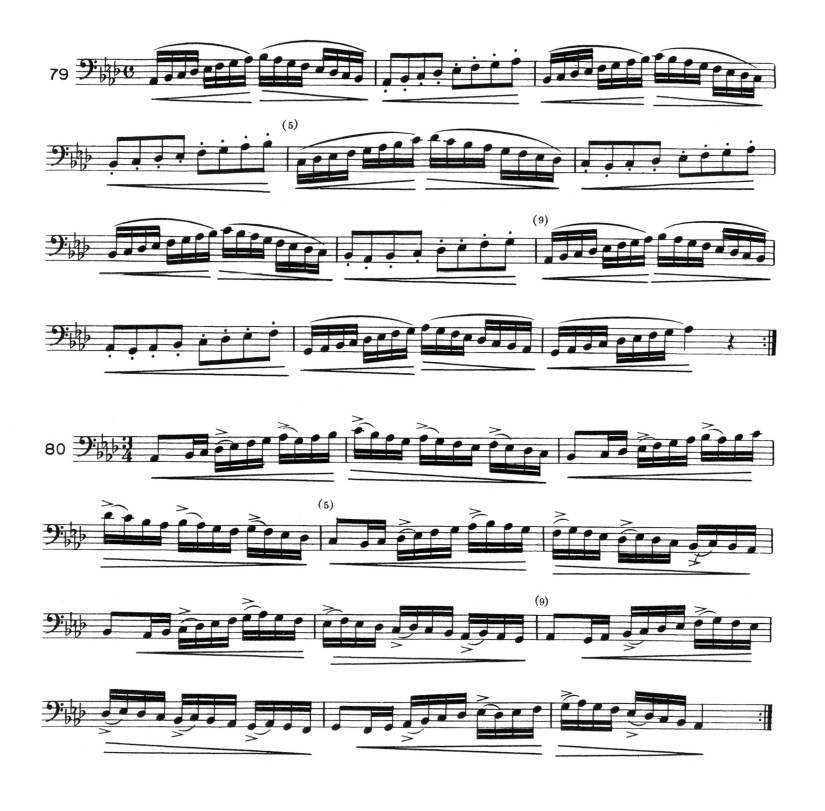

Embouchure Studies

Slur as many tones as possible. Also practice tonguing each tone.

Slur as many tones as possible. Also practice tonguing each tone.

Key of D♭ Major

Long Tones to Strengthen Lips

Also practice holding each tone for EIGHT counts
When playing long tones, practice (1) $<$ and (2) $<>$.

Embouchure Studies

Slur as many tones as possible. Also practice tonguing each tone.

Slur as many tones as possible. Also practice tonguing each tone.

Key of A Minor

(Relative to the Key of C Major)

Long Tones to Strengthen Lips

Scale of A Harmonic Minor

92

Scale of A Melodic Minor

93

Also practice holding each tone for EIGHT counts.
When playing long tones, practice (1) and (2)

94

95

Embouchure Studies

Slur as many tones as possible. Also practice tonguing each tone.

96

Slur as many tones as possible. Also practice tonguing each tone.

97

Key of D Minor

(Relative to the Key of F Major)

Long Tones to Strengthen Lips

Scale of D Harmonic Minor

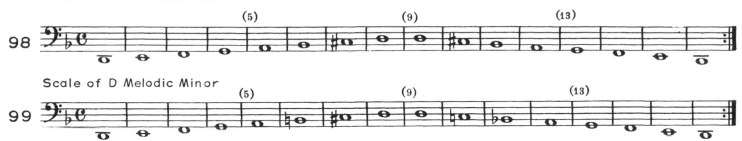

Scale of D Melodic Minor

Also practice holding each tone for EIGHT counts.
When playing long tones, practice (1) ◁ and (2) ◁▷ .

Embouchure Studies

Slur as many tones as possible. Also practice tonguing each tone.

Slur as many tones as possible. Also practice tonguing each tone.

Key of E Minor
(Relative to the Key of G Major)

Long Tones to Strengthen Lips

Scale of E Harmonic Minor

Scale of E Melodic Minor

Also practice holding each tone for EIGHT counts.
When playing long tones, practice (1) ⎯ and (2) ⎯.

Embouchure Studies

Slur as many tones as possible. Also practice tonguing each tone.

Slur as many tones as possible. Also practice tonguing each tone.

Key of G Minor
(Relative to the Key of B Major)

Long Tones to Strengthen Lips

Scale of G Harmonic Minor

110

Scale of G Melodic Minor

111

Also practice holding each tone for EIGHT counts.
When playing long tones, practice (1) $\mathrel{<\!\!\!\!=}$ and (2) $\mathrel{\cdot\!<\!\!=\!\!>}$.

112

113

Embouchure Studies

Slur as many tones as possible. Also practice tonguing each tone.

114

Slur as many tones as possible. Also practice tonguing each tone.

115

993-47

Key of B Minor

(Relative to the Key of D Major)

Long Tones to Strengthen Lips

Scale of B Harmonic Minor

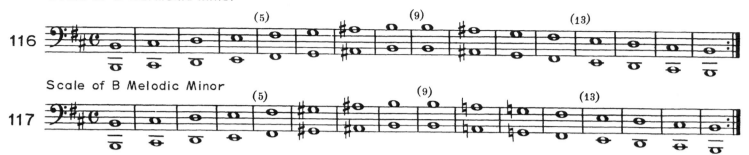

Scale of B Melodic Minor

Also practice holding each tone for EIGHT counts.
When playing long tones, practice (1) ⟨ and (2) ⟨ ⟩ .

Embouchure Studies

Slur as many tones as possible. Also practice tonguing each tone.

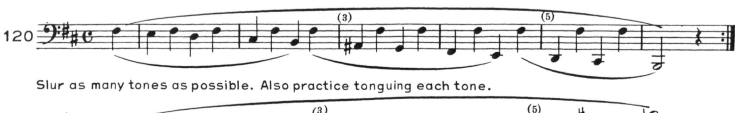

Slur as many tones as possible. Also practice tonguing each tone.

Key of C Minor
(Relative to the Key of E♭ Major)

Long Tones to Strengthen Lips

Scale of C Harmonic Minor

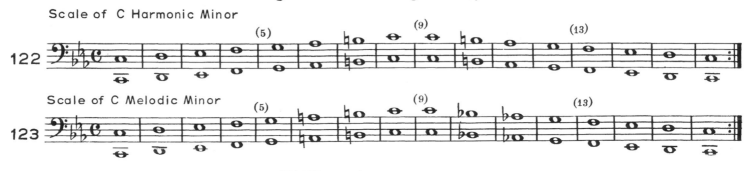

Scale of C Melodic Minor

Also practice holding each tone for EIGHT counts.
When playing long tones, practice (1) ⋍ and (2) ⋍⋍ .

Embouchure Studies

Slur as many tones as possible. Also practice tonguing each tone.

Slur as many tones as possible. Also practice tonguing each tone.

993-47

Key of F♯ Minor
(Relative to the Key of A Major)

Long Tones to Strengthen Lips

Scale of F♯ Harmonic Minor

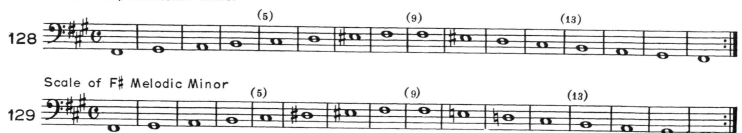

Scale of F♯ Melodic Minor

Also practice holding each tone for EIGHT counts
When playing long tones, practice (1) ⎯⎯ and (2) ⎯⎯

Embouchure Studies
Slur as many tones as possible. Also practice tonguing each tone.

Slur as many tones as possible. Also practice tonguing each tone.

Key of F Minor
(Relative to the Key of A♭ Major)

Long Tones to Strengthen Lips

Scale of **F** Harmonic Minor

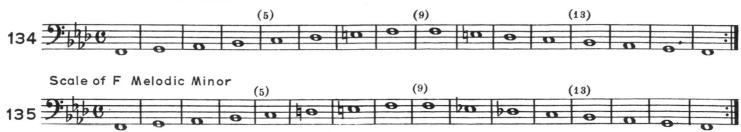

Scale of **F** Melodic Minor

Also practice holding each tone for EIGHT counts.
When playing long tones, practice (1) $<$ and (2) $<>$.

Embouchure Studies

Slur as many tones as possible. Also practice tonguing each tone.

Slur as many tones as possible. Also practice tonguing each tone.

993-47

Key of B♭ Minor
(Relative to the Key of D♭ Major)

Long Tones to Strengthen Lips

Scale of B♭ Harmonic Minor

Scale of B♭ Melodic Minor

Also practice holding each tone for EIGHT counts
When playing long tones, practice (1) $\diagdown$ and (2) $\diagdown\diagup$.

Embouchure Studies
Slur as many tones as possible. Also practice tonguing each tone.

Slur as many tones as possible. Also practice tonguing each tone.

Major Scales

Harmonic Minor Scales

Melodic Minor Scales

Arpeggios

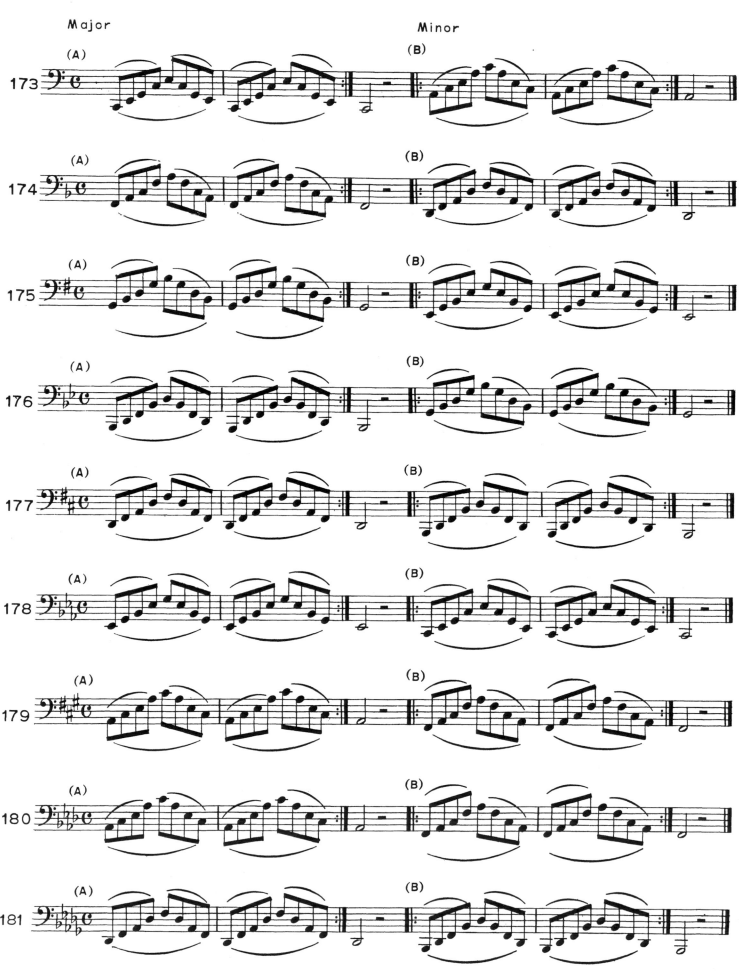

Chromatc Studies

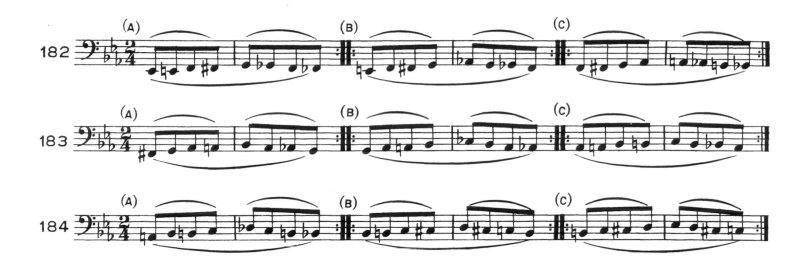

Chromatic Studies in Sixteenth Notes

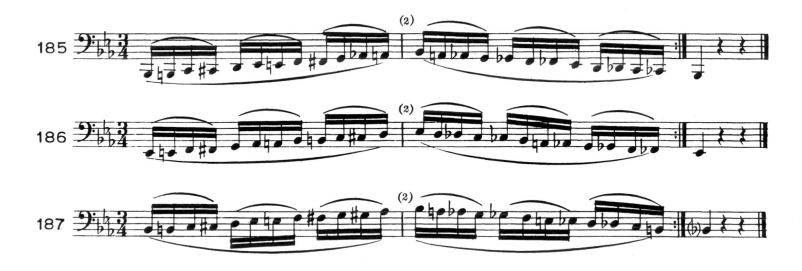

Chromatic Studies in Triplets

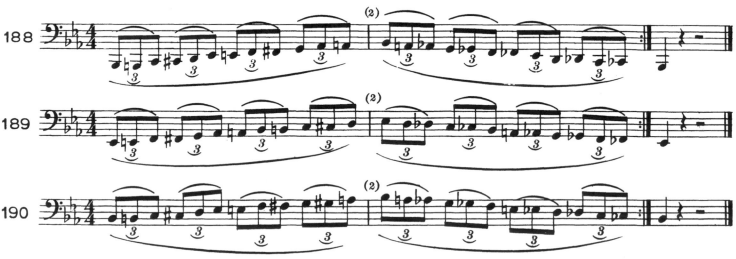

Chromatic Scales

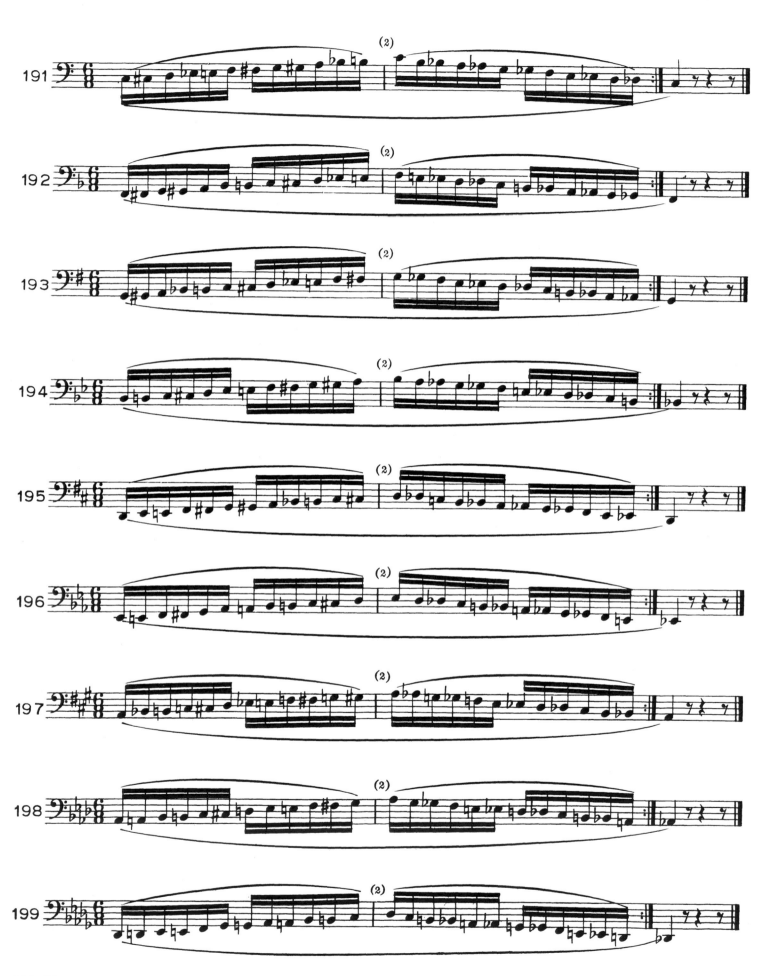

Basic Exercises to Develop Tones

Basic Exercises to Strengthen Tones

(a) Also practice very slowly, holding each tone for (1) FOUR counts, and (2) EIGHT counts.
When playing long tones, practice (1) ⟨ and (2) ⟨ ⟩.
(b) Also practice very legato (1) slurring each two tones, and (2) slurring each four tones.

Studies in Mechanism

Interval Exercises

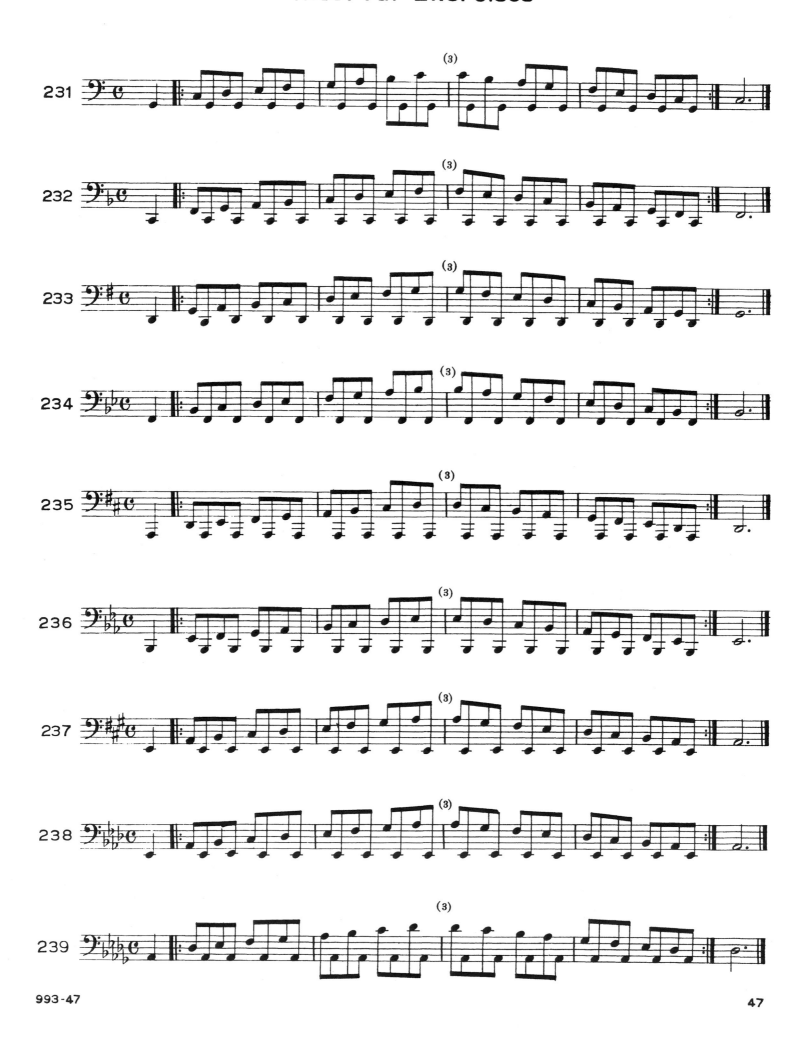

Technic Builder No.1

Technic Builder No.2

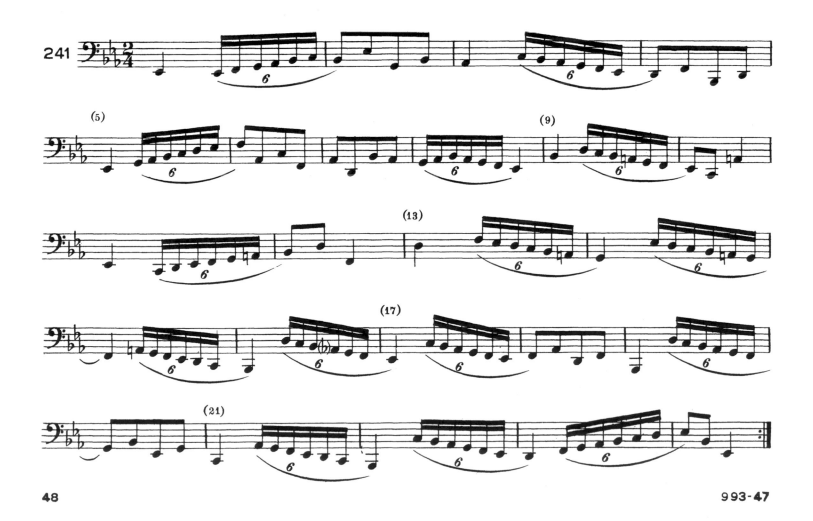